Pandemic planet

ANNA CLAYBOURNE

W
FRANKLIN WATTS
LONDON • SYDNEY

Franklin Watts
First published in Great Britain in 2021 by the Watts Publishing Group
Copyright © the Watts Publishing Group 2021

Editor: Julia Bird
Designer: Rocket Design (East Anglia) Ltd

Alamy: bg3112/Stockimo 40c; BSIP SA 38bc; Chronicle 10t; Everett Collection Historical 37tl; Incamerastock 10bl; Interfoto 37tr; Fei Maohua/Xinhua 24t;Niday Picture Library 11t; North Wind Picture Archives 31c; Science History Images 38bl; Vintage Space 23br; Li Ye/Xinhua 19b.
Getty Images: AFP 17b.
Science Photo Library: NIAID/National Institutes of Health 4t.Shutterstock: Ad libitum 7br; Ali_shh_a 30t; Ankomando 9br; Archivector 15cl; ArtMari 35tr; Angelina Bambina 5tr, 22cr; Basel101658 15c; Big Stocker 32cl; Blueastro 22cl; Olga W Boeva 28c; BOLDG 18t; Corona Borealis Studio 26b; Dennis Cristo 39t; CRStocker 5b; Curiousity 25b; Dedhik 15t; Draftfolio 35cl; Ducu59us 36c; Elegant Solution 24br; Eveleen 14c; Everett Collection 7t,11b, 13b, 20c; FOS ICON 32cr; Gate Out 32bcr; Gmarc 8cr,41b; GoodStudio 22t, 24bl,34b,37b,41tl; Grinbox 17tl, 23cl; Pierrette Guertin 6t; Matt Gush 27b;IMissisHope 9t; In-Finity 14b; inkheartX 33t; Inspiring 41cr; Invector 42c; Jesadaphorn 24bc; Katykin 12-13; Kateryna Kon 8tr; La1n 23tl; Nasi Lemak 7bl;Lightly Stranded 16c; light_s 34c; Limolida Design Studio 19t; Lukmanhakim 32br; LynxVector 9cr; Madua 17tr; Magnia 21tbg; Marish 27,42br; zizi_mentos 35tcr; MicroOne 6c,8br, 29t; Miki022 9cl;Millering 31b; Anna Minkina 30bl; Musmellow 32bcl; MyCreative 26t; Lia Nanuk 6b; Anastasia Ni 43b; noEnde 29c; OlyaOK 23cr; Art_OLD 26-27bg; Paranyu 9bl, 26br; Channarong Pherngjanda 10br; Philia 32crc; Pixsooz 25t; Rassco 5tl; RedKoala 29b; Sensvector 21b;Shaineast 32-33 bg; Siberian Art 4b; Alexander Smulskiy 20-21b; Solomon7 15cr, 15b; ST.art 5c, 22b; Tartila 8bl; TeddyandMia 40b;TeraVector 23tr; TheModernCanvas 32clc;Tn-prints 42bl; Piotr Urakau 32bl; Vectors Bang 31t; Vidoslava 42b; Visual Generation 35cr; WinWin artlab 18b; ya_blue_ko 30br; Fatmawati achmad zaenuri 28b.
Wellcome Collection: CCBY 4.0 23bc

Every effort has been made to clear copyright. Should there be any inadvertent omission, please apply to the publisher for rectification.

ISBN: 978 1 4451 8070 0

Printed in Dubai

Franklin Watts
An imprint of
Hachette Children's Group
Part of the Watts Publishing Group
Carmelite House
50 Victoria Embankment
London EC4Y 0DZ

An Hachette UK Company
www.hachettechildrens.co.uk
www.franklinwatts.co.uk

– Contents –

Worldwide crisis

In early 2020, a deadly new disease began to spread around the world, passing from person to person. The disease was caused by a type of germ called a coronavirus, and scientists gave it the name COVID-19.

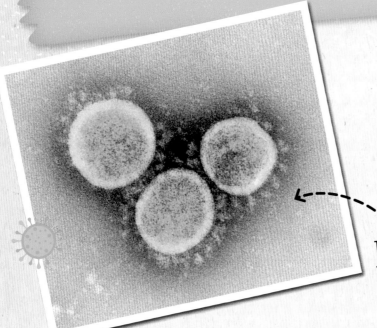

The coronavirus germs that cause COVID-19.

COVID-19 STANDS FOR CORONAVIRUS DISEASE 2019 (THE YEAR IT WAS FIRST DESCRIBED).

PANDEMIC PLANET

As the COVID-19 virus infected more and more people, and reached almost every part of the planet, it became known as a pandemic – a disease outbreak that affects many countries, or even the whole world.

Besides making millions of people sick, and causing a lot of deaths, a pandemic has other effects too, as people try to avoid catching the disease and stop it from spreading,

These can include:

★ Banning meet-ups and crowds – so no weddings or parties!

★ Cancelling concerts, festivals and sporting events.

★ Closing shops, cafes and bars.

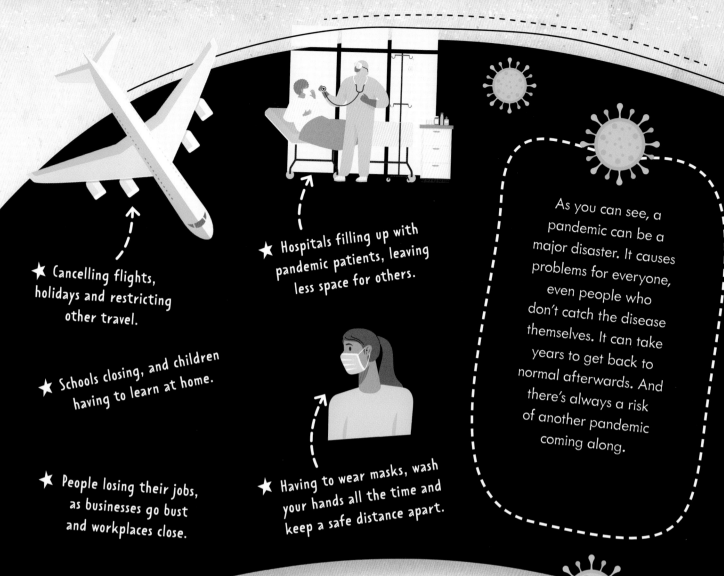

★ Cancelling flights, holidays and restricting other travel.

★ Schools closing, and children having to learn at home.

★ People losing their jobs, as businesses go bust and workplaces close.

★ Hospitals filling up with pandemic patients, leaving less space for others.

★ Having to wear masks, wash your hands all the time and keep a safe distance apart.

As you can see, a pandemic can be a major disaster. It causes problems for everyone, even people who don't catch the disease themselves. It can take years to get back to normal afterwards. And there's always a risk of another pandemic coming along.

★ Stop germs from spreading.

WHAT CAN WE DO?

TO FIGHT PANDEMICS, WE NEED TO:

★ Find medicines to treat new diseases.

★ Prevent diseases from turning into pandemics in the first place.

THIS BOOK EXPLAINS HOW WE CAN DO THAT — AND WHAT YOU CAN DO TO HELP.

What is a pandemic?

Pandemic can be a confusing word, as it sounds similar to other words. What's the difference between a pandemic and an epidemic? And what about 'endemic'?

PAN meaning 'all'

DĒMOS meaning 'nation' or 'people'

ALL THE PEOPLE

The word pandemic comes from two ancient Greek words:

So a pandemic is a disease that spreads all over the world, or across multiple countries or continents, affecting a large number of people.

PASSING IT ON

Appendicitis

The name pandemic is usually used for infectious diseases, caused by germs that pass from one person to another.

So, for example, appendicitis is NOT a pandemic, even though anyone in the world can get it. That's because it's not spread by germs, and it's quite rare.

But when a new germ, such as the COVID-19 virus, spreads rapidly around the globe and makes lots of people seriously ill, that's a pandemic.

EPIDEMICS

An epidemic is like a pandemic, but smaller and more local. It comes from the ancient Greek words 'epi' and 'dēmos', meaning 'among the people'. In an epidemic, a lot of people catch a disease and get sick, but mostly in one country or region.

For example, in 1707, a smallpox epidemic in Iceland killed over 18,000 people. Smallpox was a deadly disease that often caused epidemics in the past, but it has now been wiped out.

Smallpox was eventually eradicated by vaccination programmes, such as this one in New York, USA, in 1872.

ENDEMIC

Finally, the word 'endemic' describes something that belongs to a particular place. Diseases can be endemic. Sleeping sickness, for example, a disease spread by flies, is endemic to Africa.

AFRICA

Area affected by sleeping sickness

Endemic can be used to describe other things too, such as animals. For example, kangaroos are endemic to Australia, meaning that's the only place they come from.

— Germs and diseases —

Why do pandemics and epidemics exist at all?
The answer is germs, and the way they cause disease.
If a germ can be passed from one person to another,
it can cause a pandemic.

WHAT ARE GERMS?

Germs are tiny living things, or microorganisms. Like all living things, they need food and a place to live. For germs, that means living on, or inside, another living thing.

Unfortunately for us, when germs invade or infect our bodies, they can cause disease. Here's one example...

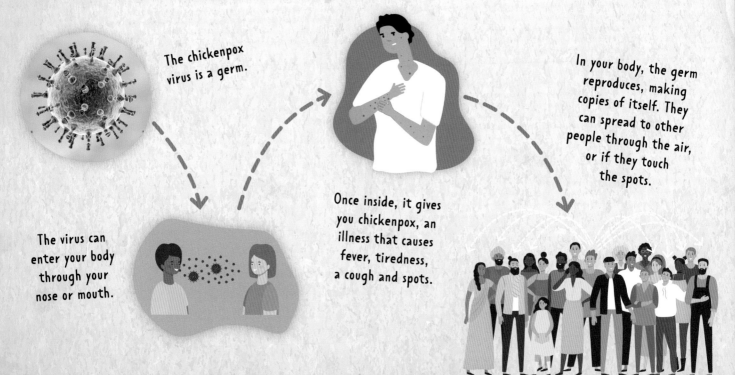

The chickenpox virus is a germ.

The virus can enter your body through your nose or mouth.

Once inside, it gives you chickenpox, an illness that causes fever, tiredness, a cough and spots.

In your body, the germ reproduces, making copies of itself. They can spread to other people through the air, or if they touch the spots.

TYPES OF GERM

There are several different types of germ.

BACTERIA
are microscopic
single-celled
creatures.

▶ **VIRUSES**
are tiny, much smaller
than bacteria. They
live by invading cells.

▶ **FUNGI**
Some types
of fungi are
germs too.

▶ **PROTOZOA**
are microscopic
animals that act
as germs.

Not all bacteria, viruses, fungi and protozoa are germs – only those that cause disease. For example, some bacteria are helpful, such as Bifidobacteria. They live in our intestines, helping us to digest food, and are found in yoghurt.

HOW GERMS SPREAD

There are thousands of different disease germs. Each disease has its own particular germ, and its own ways of spreading.

GERM ▼	TYPE OF GERM ▼	WAYS IT SPREADS ▼
Influenza (flu)	Virus	Coughing, sneezing or talking
Measles	Virus	Coughing and sneezing
Malaria	Protozoan	Mosquito bites
AIDS	Virus	Blood transfusions, shared needles, sexual activity
Zika	Virus	Mosquito bites, blood transfusions, sexual activity
Sleeping sickness	Protozoan	Tsetse fly bites
Bubonic plague	Bacteria	Flea bites, coughing or touching
Lyme disease	Bacteria	Tick bites
Cholera	Bacteria	In water or food
Coronavirus	Virus	Coughing, sneezing and touching

Pandemics of the past

Pandemics and epidemics are not new — they have happened throughout human history. This timeline shows just a few of the most deadly pandemics and plagues of the past.

ANTONINE PLAGUE

Disease: Possibly smallpox

Death toll: Around 5 million

This pandemic ravaged the Roman Empire, affecting North Africa, Europe and western Asia.

165–180 CE

430–427 BCE

PLAGUE OF ATHENS

Disease: Possibly typhus

Death toll: Up to 100,000

An ancient pandemic that spread across North Africa and Europe, devastating the city-state of Athens in ancient Greece.

FIRST CONTACT

From the late 15th century, explorers and invaders crossed the Atlantic from Europe to the Americas, taking disease germs with them and causing deadly pandemics.

16TH CENTURY

NEW WORLD PANDEMICS

Disease: Smallpox and others

Death toll: Around 56 million

Diseases taken to the Americas by European invaders kill over 90% of the native people.

THE GREAT PLAGUES

Disease: Bubonic plague

Death toll: Over 3 million

Bubonic plague pandemics hit many parts of Africa, Asia and Europe in the 17th century.

17TH CENTURY

PLAGUE OF JUSTINIAN

Disease: Bubonic plague

Death toll: Around 30 million

The first bubonic plague pandemic, spreading through Europe and the Mediterranean region.

541–542 CE

THE BLACK DEATH

Disease: Bubonic plague

Death toll: Up to 200 million

The deadliest pandemic in history, when bubonic plague raged through Asia, Africa and Europe (see pages 12–13).

1346–1353

SMALLER PANDEMICS

Long ago, most people didn't travel much, and some parts of the world were completely cut off from each other. So early pandemics didn't spread all over the world, as they can today.

DEADLY DISEASES

Just a few diseases have been responsible for huge numbers of deaths throughout history.

Malaria	up to 50 billion
Smallpox	up to 500 million
Plague	up to 250 million
Flu	up to 50 million
Cholera	up to 40 million

FLU PANDEMIC

Disease: Influenza (flu)

Death toll: Up to 50 million

This deadly flu pandemic began at the end of the First World War (1914–1918) and spread around the world (see pages 20–21).

THIRD CHOLERA PANDEMIC

Disease: Cholera

Death toll: Over 1 million

The worst of several cholera pandemics, affecting Asia, Africa, Europe and North America.

1846–1860

1918–1919

— The Black Death —

The Black Death, which struck Asia, Africa and Europe in the 14th century, was the worst pandemic in history. Most scientists think it was caused by a disease called bubonic plague.

PLAGUE PANDEMICS

The first known bubonic plague pandemic was the Plague of Justinian, in 541 CE. Since then, the disease has caused many more pandemics. Historians divide them into three main waves:

YEAR
▼

300

400

500

600

700

800

900

1000

1100

1200

1300

1400

1500

1600

1700

1800

1900

2000

First wave
541–549

The Black Death
(1346–1353) was
the start of the
second wave.

Second wave
1340s–1830s

Third wave
1855–1945

PATH OF THE PLAGUE

The Black Death pandemic probably began in Mongolia or China in the early 1340s. From there, it spread across Asia and parts of Africa along trading routes. In 1347, sailing ships took the disease with them from the Black Sea to Sicily, and from there it spread all over Europe and the surrounding area.

RATS AND FLEAS

Bubonic plague is caused by a type of bacteria. It's found in small mammals, such as rats, and can spread to humans when fleas bite rats and then bite people. It can also spread from person to person in flea bites, in the air or by touching an infected person.

KEY TO MAP

 = major outbreaks

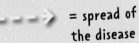 = spread of the disease

WHAT WAS IT LIKE?

Having the plague was horrible! The symptoms included fever and shivering, headache, vomiting, and painful swellings called buboes. Some people survived, but many died within days.

— Immunity —

We're always surrounded by germs, yet pandemics only happen once in a while. This is because the human body has an immune system, which can usually fight off germs.

THE IMMUNE SYSTEM

The immune system has many parts. Some stop germs from getting in, while others kill germs inside the body. For example...

Earwax traps germs.

Saliva, tears and sweat contain germ-killing chemicals.

Blood contains white blood cells that kill germs.

Mucus in the nose, throat and lungs traps germs.

Stomach acid kills germs.

LEARNING ABOUT GERMS

When a new disease germ infects the body, some white blood cells learn to recognise it, and make chemicals called antibodies to attack it.

Usually, the white cells then remember that germ, so that if it invades again, they can find it and kill it straight away. This makes your body immune to that disease, meaning it can fight it off. For example, if you've had chickenpox, you are probably immune to it, and won't get it again.

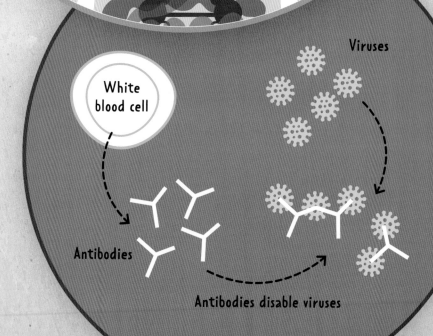

Viruses

White blood cell

Antibodies

Antibodies disable viruses

VACCINATIONS

Vaccinations work in the same way. They contain germs with some parts removed, so they don't cause the disease, but the immune system still learns to recognise and kill the real disease germs.

Vaccinations can protect against many diseases, such as measles and mumps.

CHANGING GERMS

There are lots of disease germs around, but most people have some immunity to them. We might catch flu, colds or stomach bugs, but our bodies usually fight them off in a few days.

However, like other living things, germs can change over time. Sometimes, this creates a new form, or strain, of a germ, especially if the germ passes from animals to humans. As people are not immune to this new strain, it spreads easily and can make people very sick — and that can lead to a pandemic.

The flu virus is an example of a germ that evolves fast, and often evolves new strains.

New flu strain

— The early stages —

At the start of a pandemic, it can be hard to tell what's happening. Usually, we only know a new, dangerous germ has come along when people start to get sick from it.

NOTICING SOMETHING NEW

The first people to spot a new germ are usually hospital doctors. They see lots of unwell people every day, so they know when something changes. They might notice...

★ More patients than usual going to hospital

★ Lots of people with the same symptoms

★ People getting more sick than usual

★ More people dying than usual

★ A pattern, such as an illness affecting a particular age group.

1

NEW GERM ALERT!

If a hospital suspects a new germ, it reports it to the government. Governments around the world have pandemic action plans, so that they can act as fast as possible when this happens. They alert other hospitals to look out for new cases, and call in expert scientists to study the germ.

② WHAT IS IT?

The scientists look at the germ under a microscope to identify it. What type of germ is it? Is it a new strain of a disease such as flu, or a whole new disease?

③ HOW DOES IT SPREAD?

Scientists look at where patients have been, and how they might have caught the germ. Does it spread through the air, or maybe in water? Is it linked to a particular workplace, or a type of animal?

⑤ STOPPING THE SPREAD

At this stage, a pandemic could still be prevented, using emergency measures such as:

★ Keeping patients with the germ in separate hospital wards

★ Using protective gear to keep health workers safe

★ Testing everyone a patient has been in contact with

★ Quarantining people who enter a country, which means keeping them isolated for a while to check if they have the disease.

④ MAKING A TEST

Scientists use the germ's genetic code (the parts inside it that make it work) to design a test for the disease.

There have been several outbreaks of the deadly disease Ebola in Africa, but emergency measures stopped them from becoming pandemics.

— Out of control —

If a disease outbreak isn't stopped in time, it can spread so fast and far that it's impossible to keep track of it. When it affects lots of countries and a large number of people, it may be officially declared a pandemic.

SPREADING OUT

Usually, a new disease appears in one place, then spreads out from there, carried by people who may or may not be aware that they are infected, travelling from place to place.

PANDEMIC FACTORS

Lots of things affect how fast a germ spreads, and how likely it is to cause a pandemic. Germs usually spread faster...

★ In big cities, where lots of people travel around to go to work and meet friends

★ If they can be passed from person to person through the air

★ In places with crowded living conditions

★ In places that don't have good sanitation (clean running water and flushing toilets).

The Ⓡ number

In a pandemic, the R number, or reproduction number, is important. It shows how many people each person with the disease passes it on to.

If R is 3, for example, each person with the disease passes it onto 3 others – and the number of people with the disease will rise very quickly.

THE WHO

The WHO, or World Health Organization, is an international organisation that aims to improve health around the world. It announces when a disease outbreak has become a pandemic. It also issues advice, and keeps track of the spread of the disease and the number of deaths.

WHO director-general Dr Tedros Adhanom makes an announcement during the coronavirus pandemic.

The 1918-19 flu pandemic

The 1918-19 flu pandemic, also known as the Spanish Flu, was the deadliest flu pandemic in history. It was also the worst pandemic of modern times.

HOW IT STARTED

No one knows where the pandemic began, but a new type of flu was first reported in early 1918, when it began spreading among soldiers at a training camp in Kansas, USA. By July 1918, it had reached the rest of the Americas, Europe, Asia and Australia.

1918 was the last year of the First World War, which made the pandemic worse. Soldiers moving around the world took the virus with them, and it spread fast in crowded war hospitals and army camps.

WAS IT SPANISH?

No! Spanish Flu was only called this because it was first reported in Spanish newspapers. In fact, scientists still aren't sure exactly where it came from — it could have been somewhere in Europe, America or Asia.

A nurse and a flu patient in India during the Spanish Flu pandemic

PANDEMIC WAVES

The 1918 flu pandemic came in waves, getting worse, then better, then worse again. This often happens in pandemics when the virus spreads to new areas, or people relax and stop taking care to avoid infection. Flu also spreads more easily in winter, so that can cause a new wave too.

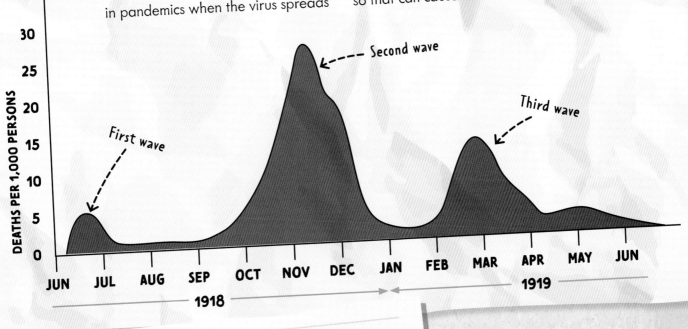

DEATHS PER 1,000 PERSONS

First wave

Second wave

Third wave

JUN JUL AUG SEP OCT NOV DEC JAN FEB MAR APR MAY JUN

1918

1919

The symptoms

Different strains of flu can have slightly different symptoms. In 1918, many patients developed pneumonia, where the lungs get infected and fill up with fluid, making it hard to breathe. This made the 1918 flu unusually deadly.

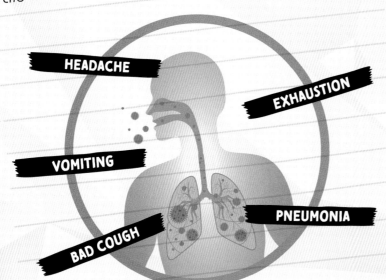

HEADACHE

EXHAUSTION

VOMITING

PNEUMONIA

BAD COUGH

SPANISH FLU FACTS

★ The 1918 flu infected around 500 million people around the world.

★ Up to 50 million people died – around 10% of those who caught it.

★ The pandemic killed more people than the First World War itself.

21

— Lockdown! —

During a pandemic, governments try to stop the disease from spreading. One way to do this is by ordering a lockdown — closing public places and making people stay at home.

If a disease can be passed on through the air or by touching, a lockdown is a good way to stop it spreading. People have to stay mostly indoors, so they can't meet up and pass the germ around.

LOCKDOWN LIFE

★ Places where people meet up or crowd together are closed.

★ Most offices are closed and people have to work from home if they can.

★ Schools close and children have to do schoolwork at home.

Masks help to stop germs from spreading.

PEOPLE HAVE TO KEEP AWAY FROM EACH OTHER, KNOWN AS SOCIAL DISTANCING

◀ 2 METRES ▶

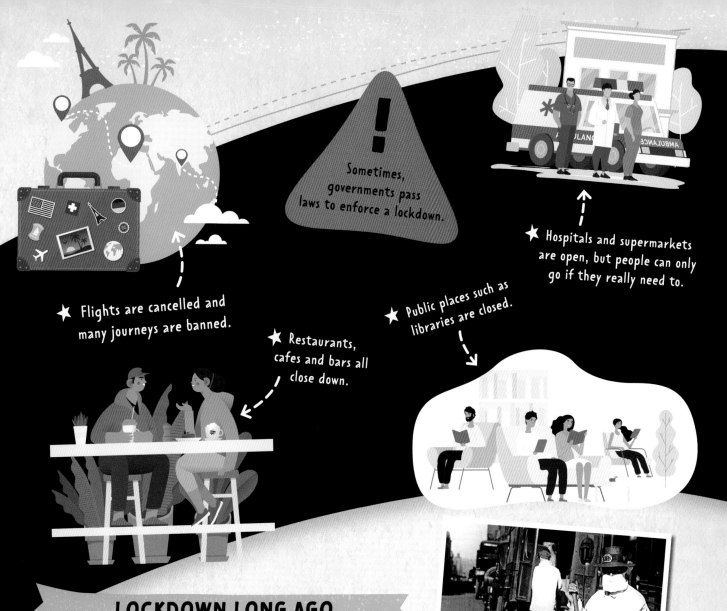

Sometimes, governments pass laws to enforce a lockdown.

★ Hospitals and supermarkets are open, but people can only go if they really need to.

★ Flights are cancelled and many journeys are banned.

★ Restaurants, cafes and bars all close down.

★ Public places such as libraries are closed.

LOCKDOWN LONG AGO

Lockdowns, masks and social distancing have been used for centuries during pandemics.

From the 1630s, doctors wore beaked masks to visit plague patients. They were filled with herbs and spices, which were believed to protect them from the disease.

In 1665, bubonic plague hit London, England. A parcel from London brought the disease to Eyam in Derbyshire. The villagers agreed that no one would be allowed to leave or enter the village. Three-quarters of villagers died, but their actions helped stop the plague's spread.

A 17th century doctor wearing a plague mask and protective clothes. He carries a cane to point to and examine patients' bodies without having to touch them.

During the 1918 flu pandemic, there was a strict lockdown in New York, USA.

These men are wearing masks to disinfect the empty streets.

— Pandemic problems —

Of course, a pandemic is in itself a huge problem, as lots of people get sick, and some die. But it can also lead to a range of other problems.

HEALTH CRISIS

Pandemic patients often have to go to hospital, and there might not be enough hospital beds for everyone. There could also be shortages of medicine, equipment and hospital staff.

On top of this, people still get other illnesses and injuries. But if hospitals are full, it's hard for them to get treatment. And some may be scared to go to hospital, in case they catch the illness there. This leads to more people dying of other causes, as well as the pandemic disease itself.

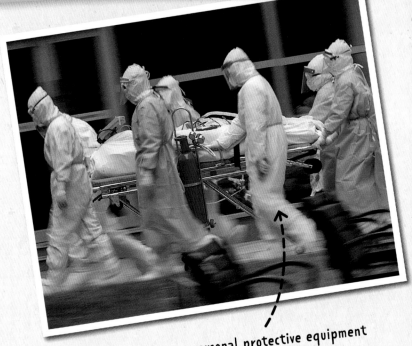

Hospital staff wear personal protective equipment (PPE) to protect themselves against germs.

PANDEMIC POVERTY

Pandemics are very bad for the economy — the system of money and wealth. In a healthy economy, most people are working, earning and spending, and there's enough money for everyone. People also pay taxes to the government, to spend on things like hospitals, schools and welfare benefits.

Money constantly moves around as people work, get paid and buy things.

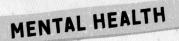

All these factors can affect people's mental health too, making them feel stressed, anxious or depressed.

So can being stuck at home during a lockdown.

She's getting on my nerves!

I miss my friends. I'm scared we'll get sick...

I can't help with schoolwork and do my job too!

How long is this going to go on?

If I don't work we'll have no money...

But in a pandemic, businesses close and events get cancelled. People lose their jobs, and businesses go bust. Lots of people now have no job and no money to spend – so everyone is poorer.

If someone cancels a big wedding, for example, lots of businesses lose money and people lose work.

HOTEL VENUE

DRESS SHOP

CATERING COMPANY

WAITERS

BAND

FLOWERS

The COVID-19 pandemic

At the end of 2019, doctors in Wuhan, China, reported early signs of a new, dangerous disease. In the next few months, the disease, named COVID-19, became a worldwide pandemic.

WHAT IS COVID-19?

COVID-19 is a respiratory disease, meaning it affects the breathing system. Most people who catch it only have a mild illness. But some develop pneumonia (see page 21) or organ failure (when body organs stop working).

Wuhan `--->`

THE VIRUS

COVID-19 is caused by a coronavirus. There are several different types of coronavirus, which cause different diseases, including common colds. The COVID-19 virus is a new type that probably developed sometime in 2019.

COMMON SYMPTOMS OF COVID-19:

FEVER

EXHAUSTION

CONSTANT COUGH

SHORTNESS OF BREATH

LOSS OF SENSE OF SMELL AND TASTE

Coronavirus means 'crown virus'. Coronaviruses have little sticking-out parts all over them, like the spikes on a crown.

PROGRESS OF A PANDEMIC

By the end of January 2020, the new coronavirus had spread to more than 20 countries around the world. Doctors and scientists discovered that:

☀ COVID-19 is most dangerous for older people, and those who have other illnesses or health conditions, such as diabetes.

☀ The virus spreads in the air when people cough and talk, and when they touch infected people or contaminated surfaces.

☀ About 1% of people infected with COVID-19 die.

☀ Some people with the virus have no symptoms, but can still infect others.

World lockdown

To combat the pandemic, countries introduced lockdowns and began testing programs to keep track of the disease. Some countries, such as New Zealand and Vietnam, managed to keep the number of cases and deaths very low. Others, such as Brazil and the USA, had high infection rates and hundreds of thousands of deaths.

Some countries saw demonstrations against lockdowns and mask-wearing.

COVID-19 TIMELINE

2019
29 Dec: First reports of the new disease

2020
9 Jan: First COVID-19 death

Jan-Mar: COVID-19 spreads beyond China to Europe, the Americas, Australia and Africa

6 Mar: Cases worldwide pass 100,000

11 Mar: WHO declares COVID-19 a pandemic

3 Apr: Cases worldwide pass 1 million

10 Apr: Deaths worldwide pass 100,000

28 Jun: Cases worldwide pass 10 million

14 Jul: Early tests on vaccines show some success

24 Aug: The COVAX organisation is set up to help countries share vaccines

18 Sep: Cases worldwide pass 30 million

28 Sep: Deaths worldwide pass 1 million

October: Many countries report a second wave of infections

9 Nov: Tests show Covid vaccines are effective

25 Nov: Cases worldwide pass 60 million

Dec: Covid-19 spreading faster, due to new forms of the virus

8 Dec: Vaccination of the public begins

2021
15 Jan: Deaths worldwide pass 2 million

Jan-Apr: More vaccines are developed, and vaccination programs continue around the world

17 Apr: Deaths worldwide pass 3 million

30 Apr: Cases worldwide pass 150 million

April-May: Vaccination programs slow the pandemic, but many countries still have rising numbers of cases

— Finding a solution —

During a pandemic, scientists, doctors and governments work together to develop tests for the disease, and to look for treatments, cures and vaccines.

TESTING AND TRACING

To try to limit the spread of the germ, governments use testing and tracing. This means that if someone has a positive test, meaning they have the germ, everyone they have been in close contact with has to stay away from others, or self-isolate, and have a test if they start to show any symptoms.

To test for coronavirus, a nurse takes a swab from inside your nose and throat. This is then tested for the virus.

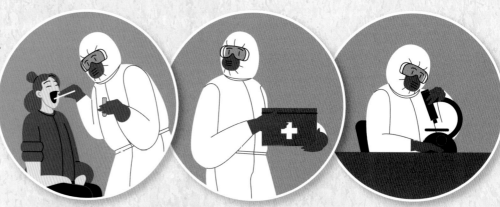

This person has a positive test, meaning they have the germ and must stay away from others.

Everyone they have been in close contact with must also self-isolate and get tested if they show symptoms.

Other people are now less likely to catch the germ.

TREATMENTS AND CURES

As a pandemic goes on, doctors try out different treatments and develop new ones. For example, when the AIDS virus first spread in the 1980s, there were no treatments. But now there are medicines that can allow AIDS patients to stay healthy and live a normal life.

Since the 1940s, we have been using medicines called antibiotics, which kill bacteria (see page 36). They help to control bacterial diseases like bubonic plague and cholera, which once caused pandemics.

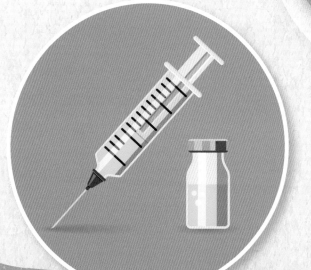

THE RACE FOR A VACCINE

Meanwhile, scientists use the pandemic disease germ to make a vaccine (see page 15). This can take months or even years, because vaccines have to be carefully tested. Once the vaccine is ready, it's used to protect people from the disease, helping to end the pandemic.

GOODBYE SMALLPOX

The deadly disease smallpox killed millions of people in the past. But from the 1950s onwards, a worldwide vaccination program made the virus rarer and rarer, and by 1980 it had been wiped out.

— Back to normal —

As some people recover from the disease, and others start being vaccinated, a pandemic gradually comes to an end. But it can still take a while for life to get back to normal.

JOBS AND MONEY

Once it's safe, shops, cafes and other public places can reopen. But they can only reopen if they still exist. In a pandemic, businesses often can't survive and have to shut down permanently, leaving lots of people unemployed. So it can take longer for new businesses to start up, and for people to find new jobs.

LONG-TERM EFFECTS

Pandemics are bad for people's health, even if they don't catch the pandemic disease itself. Problems like these can continue after a pandemic:

★ Poverty increases, which can lead to illnesses caused by poor diet or low-quality housing.

★ A pandemic can leave people with mental illnesses, such as anxiety about going outside.

★ Some people are suffering from grief and depression after losing loved ones.

★ If a country's economy is badly damaged, there's not much money for healthcare.

A HELPING HAND

If governments have enough money, they can set up schemes to try to get the economy going again. For example, a government could give out grants to help people start new businesses, or give people vouchers to spend in cafes.

However, this means that wealthier countries can recover more quickly – while poorer ones suffer for longer.

CHANGING THE WORLD

Sometimes, a pandemic can change things permanently.

After the Black Death, (see pages 12–13), so many people had died that there was a shortage of farm workers. From then on, workers could demand better pay and treatment from landowners.

A 14th-century farm worker

After the 1918–19 flu pandemic (see pages 20–21), governments realised that they needed better healthcare. This led to the launch of national health and welfare systems in many countries.

—Pandemic preparation—

Even before COVID-19, experts knew a big pandemic was likely to happen. The way germs work means there could always be a pandemic around the corner. How can we make sure we're ready for it?

ON THE ALERT!

To catch a pandemic germ early, we need alert systems for reporting new germs and diseases, and expert scientists who can study them. The WHO already does this, but the world has to keep making sure that as many countries as possible are on board.

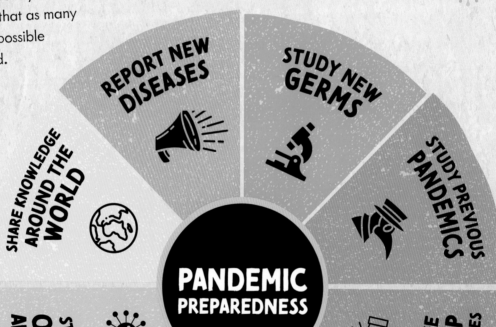

PANDEMIC PREPAREDNESS

REPORT NEW DISEASES

STUDY NEW GERMS

STUDY PREVIOUS PANDEMICS

ENCOURAGE FRIENDSHIP BETWEEN COUNTRIES

TREAT EXISTING DISEASES TO MAKE POPULATIONS HEALTHIER

KEEP HEALTH SYSTEMS WORKING WELL

STORE DATA ON GERMS AND DISEASES

SHARE KNOWLEDGE AROUND THE WORLD

BUILDING SUPPLIES

In a pandemic, hospitals need extra medicines, equipment, cleaning materials and protective clothing. So it's important to build up emergency supplies of these things to use when a pandemic strikes.

During the COVID-19 pandemic, some countries ran out of personal protective equipment, such as masks, gloves, and germ-proof gowns and aprons. Without them, health workers were more likely to catch the disease from their patients.

ANIMAL HEALTH

When a new, dangerous germ appears, it often comes from animals. For example, the plague was spread by rodents, and new flu strains have come from pigs and birds. So another way to be prepared is to help people who work with animals to stay safe – for example by setting up clear systems and rules for hygiene, animal care and reporting new diseases.

As germs evolve, they can sometimes move from animals to humans.

FACT FILE

The germs most likely to cause pandemics:

★ Flu virus

★ Coronaviruses

★ Haemorrhagic viruses, such as Ebola, Marburg virus and Lassa fever

★ Nipah virus

★ Rift Valley fever

★ 'Disease X' – any new, as-yet unknown disease.

— *What can you do?* —

Governments, scientists and the WHO all have a big part to play in preventing pandemics. But what we do matters too. Here's how you can help.

LOOK AFTER YOURSELF

The healthier people are, the harder it is for a pandemic to take hold because strong immune systems are better at fighting off germs.

A healthy diet includes things like fresh fruit and vegetables, eggs, fish, beans and yoghurt.

So, if you can:

★ Eat healthy food.

★ Get some exercise and fresh air several times a week.

★ Wash your hands after using the toilet, playing outside or touching animals...

★ ... and before preparing or eating food.

★ See a doctor if you're unwell.

★ Get the vaccinations recommended for you.

Emergency kit

When a pandemic begins, people often rush out and stock up on piles of supplies, causing shortages. To avoid this, you could keep a small box of spare stuff ready in case of an emergency lockdown, containing:

- ★ Clean, reusable face masks

- ★ Some dried and tinned food
- ★ Toilet roll

- ★ Hand sanitiser
- ★ A basic first-aid kit and medicines, such as paracetamol.

IN A PANDEMIC

If a pandemic happens, check the news regularly, and follow official advice, such as washing your hands, wearing a mask or staying indoors during a lockdown. If you can, check on friends, relatives and neighbours by phone or email to see if they're OK or need any help.

BEWARE OF FAKE NEWS!

During pandemics, there are often conspiracy theories that the disease isn't real, or rumours about home remedies or treatments that might actually be nonsense (and could in fact be harmful). So don't believe everything you hear! Check the scientific advice instead.

TRY NOT TO WORRY!

Worrying about a pandemic will just make you stressed and anxious. Remember, we live in the best possible time to deal with pandemics, as we have advanced medicines, modern health systems and the internet for staying in touch. Be sensible and safe, but don't panic!

Antibiotics alert!

Antibiotics are a type of medicine, used to kill bacteria in the body. Thanks to them, bacterial diseases like bubonic plague, cholera and leprosy can now be cured. But there's a problem...

ANTIBIOTIC RESISTANCE

Like other germs, bacteria can evolve and change over time. Sometimes, new forms of bacteria evolve that antibiotics cannot kill. They're called antibiotic-resistant bacteria.

Here's how this happens:

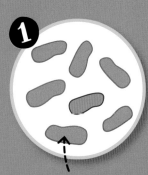

Bacteria growing in a sick person

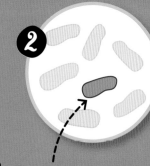

Antibiotics kill most of the bacteria – but sometimes a few stronger ones survive (especially if you stop taking the medicine too soon).

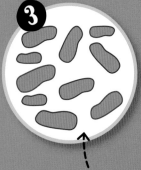

Antibiotics also kill some of the body's healthy bacteria.

Now there's space for the stronger, resistant bacteria to multiply and take over.

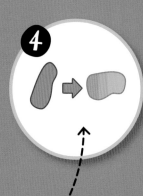

The antibiotic-resistant bacteria can spread to other people too.

What are antibiotics?

Antibiotics are bacteria-killing chemicals. They were first discovered in penicillium, a type of mould. Moulds naturally make antibiotics so they can fight off bacteria themselves.

Antibiotics have only been used in medicine for about 80 years. Before that, many more people died of bacterial diseases and infections. Today we have hundreds of different antibiotics, and manufacture them in large quantities.

Over time, you can end up with super-strong bacteria that are resistant to most antibiotics.

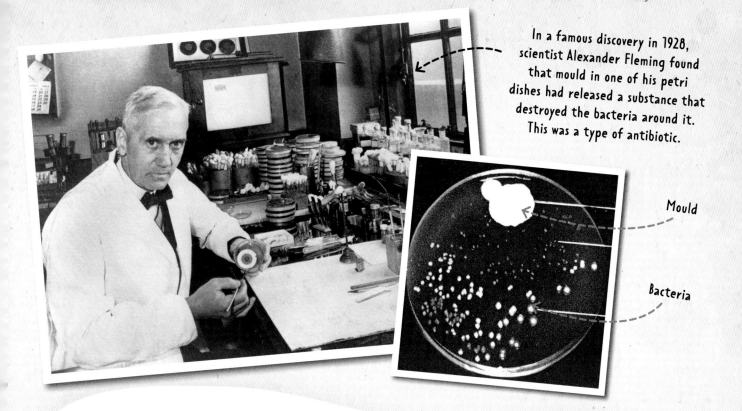

In a famous discovery in 1928, scientist Alexander Fleming found that mould in one of his petri dishes had released a substance that destroyed the bacteria around it. This was a type of antibiotic.

Mould

Bacteria

RESISTANCE PANDEMIC

Scientists are worried that eventually, a deadly, antibiotic-resistant bacterial disease could cause a pandemic. It could be a new strain of a disease like typhoid, TB (tuberculosis), cholera or even plague.

But we're working hard to try to prevent this. There are several possible solutions:

★ Finding new types of antibiotic that can kill resistant bacteria

★ Using other germs, such as viruses that attack bacteria, as a medical treatment

★ Using bacteriocins, bacteria-killing chemicals made by other bacteria.

Antibiotic-resistant TB

You might have heard of TB, or tuberculosis, but you might not realise how dangerous it is. It kills more people than any other infectious disease – and because of antibiotic resistance, this could get worse.

DEADLY DISEASE

TB is caused by bacteria. It usually damages the lungs, and sometimes other body parts too. The disease spreads when patients cough or sneeze, spreading the bacteria into the air.

Not everyone who catches the TB germ gets sick. Instead, most people get 'latent' TB, meaning they are just carrying the germ. In about one in ten people, it develops into 'active' TB. This causes symptoms like fever, sweating, weakness and coughing up blood, and can be deadly.

TB bacteria

Before antibiotics, dying of TB was very common. Victims included US president Andrew Jackson, writer Jane Austen (left), Pakistani leader Mohammed Ali Jinnah and composer Frédéric Chopin.

RICH AND POOR

Healthy people can usually fight off TB germs, and in wealthier countries, many children get TB vaccinations, so TB is rare.

However, it's more common in poorer countries. People who have poor nutrition, live in crowded conditions or already have other diseases (especially AIDS – see page 9) are more likely to catch TB.

As TB spreads through the air by coughing and sneezing, it can spread faster in cramped, crowded housing.

Treating TB

Treating TB involves taking several antibiotics over six months. Poorer people often don't get the treatment, and those who do may not complete it. This has led to new strains of antibiotic-resistant TB, which are now spreading around the world.

CAN WE FIX IT?

The WHO and other international organisations are working to develop better, quicker TB treatments for everyone who needs them, and a worldwide vaccination program. As TB is treatable and preventable, it should be possible to prevent a pandemic.

— Pandemic planet? —

Our world is changing, thanks to the activities of humans. Pollution, climate change and the growing human population are causing all kinds of problems. One of them is that they could make pandemics worse.

GLOBAL WARMING

Global warming is changing the weather. In some places, it's becoming hotter and wetter, and this can make some types of disease spread more easily.

Climate change is also making some areas dry out and become deserts, while others are damaged by windstorms and floods. This could lead to people leaving some parts of the world and looking for new places to live. This could help to spread diseases to new areas.

People living in crowded places such as refugee camps are more likely to catch diseases spread by germs.

POLLUTION

As well as causing climate change, pollution can cause smog, making it hard to breathe, especially in busy cities. Many infectious diseases, such as flu, COVID-19 and TB, affect our breathing. Polluted air makes people's lungs less healthy, so these diseases can affect them more severely.

POPULATION

Over the past 200 years, the world's human population has shot up from around 1 billion to over 7 billion. More people and bigger cities mean diseases can spread more easily.

The growing population also means humans have taken over wild habitats for our cities, roads and farms. This puts us in contact with more animals, increasing the risk of germs from animals passing to humans, and starting new pandemics.

A GREENER WORLD

We already know we need to do all we can to reverse climate change. These changes will help to protect us from pandemics too:

* Planting more trees
* Protecting animals in wildlife reserves
* Developing non-polluting energy sources, like wind, solar and wave power
* Using less polluting forms of transport, such as sailing ships and electric trains, instead of planes
* Gradually reducing the population.

— The positives —

Of course, no one wants a pandemic. They bring huge disruption, suffering and tragedy. But they can also bring some unexpected positive changes.

NEW WAYS OF WORKING

During the COVID-19 pandemic lockdowns, many people had to work from home. A lot of them found they liked it, and wanted to switch to working at home more often or even permanently. Doing this could have lots of benefits...

★ Less pollution and fewer car accidents, as fewer people are commuting

★ Less stress and more flexibility, as people can work at any time

★ Better for family life, as parents can spend more time with their children.

HAPPY WILDLIFE

During a pandemic, humans travel and go out less. There's less pollution, the air is cleaner and outdoor places are quieter. And all this is great for wildlife! Sea creatures, birds, insects and many more animals find it easier to thrive and survive. Even if this is only for a while, it helps them to breed and increase their numbers.

Busy businesses

Pandemics are usually bad for business, but some businesses can be busier than usual during a lockdown, such as:

MASK-MAKERS

LOUNGEWEAR COMPANIES

DELIVERY COMPANIES

LEARNING FROM PANDEMICS

Most importantly of all, dealing with a pandemic helps us to learn more about them, and develop new solutions.

NEW INVENTIONS

People come up with new, better designs for things like masks and medical equipment.

Scientists work on new, faster ways of making tests and vaccines.

PANDEMIC SCIENCE

We learn more about how diseases spread, and how to spot pandemics early.

We find out what works best at controlling the pandemic – lockdown, testing and tracing, social distancing, quarantine or a combination?

HUMAN BEHAVIOUR

We find out how we react to lockdown, and how to cope with it.

Experts study how crowds behave, and how to make public places safer.

All this means that we're better prepared if there is a next time.

43

— Glossary —

AIDS (Acquired Immune Deficiency Syndrome)
A type of illness spread by a virus that causes a weakened immune system.

Antibiotic A type of medicine that kills bacteria.

Antibodies Substances made by white blood cells to disable germs in the body.

Appendicitis An inflamed or infected appendix, a small body part connected to the intestines.

Bacteria Very small, single-celled microorganisms, which can sometimes act as germs.

Bacteriocins Chemicals made by some bacteria to kill other bacteria.

Black Death Another name for bubonic plague.

Bubonic plague A serious disease caused by bacteria.

Chickenpox A common disease caused by a virus, which causes spots, or pox, on the skin.

Cholera A serious disease caused by bacteria, which causes severe vomiting and diarrhoea.

Climate change A long-term change in weather patterns around the world.

Coronavirus A type of virus that can cause illnesses such as colds and COVID-19 in animals and humans.

COVID-19 A disease caused by a new type of coronavirus that first appeared in 2019.

Depression A mental illness that makes people feel sad, numb or anxious.

Diabetes An illness that makes it hard for the body to control sugar levels in the blood.

Disease X Any currently unknown disease that could cause a pandemic in the future.

Ebola A dangerous disease caused by a virus, which can cause bleeding and a fever.

Economy The system of how money circulates as things are bought and sold.

Endemic Belonging to a particular area.

Epidemic A serious outbreak of a disease in a particular area.

Flu (short for influenza) A disease caused by a virus, which can cause fever, a cough, aches and pains or pneumonia.

Fungi A group of living things that includes moulds and yeast, including some types of germ.

Germ A microorganism that can cause illnesses or infections in other living things.

Global warming A gradual increase in Earth's average temperature over the last two centuries, caused by human activities.

Habitat The natural home or surroundings of a living thing.

Immune system A body system made up of several parts that keep out and kill germs.

Immunity Protection against a disease germ, caused by the body learning how to fight it.

Infection Germs invading and growing inside the body, or a body part.

Infectious Infectious diseases can pass or spread from one person to another.

Intestines Tubes inside the body that soak up food chemicals and carry waste out of the body.

Lockdown Closing public places and making people stay at home, as a way to stop a disease from spreading.

Lyme disease An illness caused by a bacteria, spread in the bites of tiny animals called ticks.

Malaria A serious disease caused by a protozoan, and spread by mosquito bites.

Mammals A group of animals that feed their babies on milk, such as humans, pigs and cats.

Measles A disease caused by a type of virus, which causes a rash on the body.

Microorganism A very small living thing that we can only see using a microscope.

Mucus A slimy substance released by some parts of the body, such as the nose and throat.

Mumps A disease caused by a virus, which can make your face swell up.

Organs Body parts that do particular jobs, such as the heart, brain and stomach.

Pandemic A serious outbreak of a disease across a wide area, covering many countries or the whole world.

Plague Another name for bubonic plague, or sometimes used to mean any disease outbreak.

Pneumonia Infection of the lungs that can make it hard to breathe.

PPE (Personal Protective Equipment) Masks, gloves and other protective clothing used to prevent people from catching an infectious disease.

Protozoa A group of single-celled animals that can sometimes act as germs and cause diseases.

Respiratory To do with breathing, or the body parts we use for breathing.

R number The number of people that each person who has a disease passes it on to.

Rodents A group of mammals that includes mice, rats, squirrels and bats.

Saliva Another name for spit, the watery liquid in your mouth.

Sanitation Systems and equipment for keeping clean, such as running water, drains, sewers and flushing toilets.

Self-isolate Stay at home for a set period of time and avoid seeing people.

Sleeping sickness A serious disease caused by a protozoan, which causes fever, pain, confusion and sleepiness.

Smallpox A serious disease, spread by a virus, that has now been wiped out in humans.

Social distancing Keeping a minimum distance away from other people to try to stop a disease from spreading.

Spanish Flu A nickname given to a strain of flu that caused a worldwide flu pandemic in 1918–1919.

Stockpiling Keeping extra supplies of food, medicine, PPE or other things, to use in case of a pandemic or other emergency.

Strain A particular form or variety of a disease germ.

Swab A specimen of saliva, mucus or other body substance, collected by soaking it up into a piece of absorbent material, also called a swab.

Symptoms The signs and effects on the body caused by a disease.

TB (tuberculosis) A common disease spread by bacteria, which usually affects the lungs.

Typhus A disease caused by bacteria and spread in the bites of fleas, lice or mites. It causes fever, headaches and a rash.

Vaccination Teaching the body to recognise and attack a germ, by injecting or introducing a harmless version of the germ, known as a vaccine.

Wave In a pandemic, a wave is a rising number or high rate of infections.

Welfare System that provides money, healthcare, food or housing for people in need.

White blood cells Special cells found in the blood that attack, fight and destroy germs.

WHO (World Health Organization) An international organisation that exists to improve health around the world.

Wildlife reserve An area of natural habitat that is set aside and protected to allow wildlife to survive there.

Virus A type of tiny germ, much smaller than most bacteria, that reproduces by invading the cells of living things.

Zika A disease caused by a virus and usually spread by mosquitoes, that can cause fever, pain and a rash. Women who have Zika during their pregnancy may have babies with birth defects.

— Further reading —

BOOKS

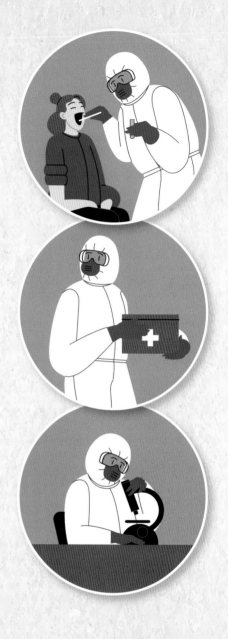

CORONAVIRUS:
A Book for Children about Covid-19
By Elizabeth Jenner (Nosy Crow, 2020)

Easy-to-understand and friendly book to answer all your questions about the COVID-19 pandemic.

PLAGUE:
A History of Pestilence and Pandemics
By Ben Hubbard (Franklin Watts, 2020)

A look back at pandemics through history, and how we have survived them.

THE GERM LAB:
The Gruesome Story of Deadly Diseases
By Richard Platt (Kingfisher, 2020)

Gruesome tales of terrible germs and the diseases and pandemics they've caused.

THE BACTERIA BOOK:
Gross Germs, Vile Viruses and Funky Fungi
By Steve Mould (Dorling Kindersley, 2018)

Fun, gross and detailed exploration of the world of germs and what they do.

WEBSITES

www.natgeokids.com/uk/discover/science/general-science/ what-is-coronavirus/

National Geographic Kids page with coronavirus facts and advice.

www.wateraid.org/uk/get-involved/teaching/hygiene-activities-for-kids

WaterAid website with activities and games about hygiene and sanitation.

www.dkfindout.com/uk/human-body/body-defences/germs-and-disease/

Interactive website on germs and diseases from DK Find Out.

www.scholastic.com/parents/school-success/learning-toolkit-blog/ germs-for-kids.html

Make a zoo of modelling-clay microorganisms.

www.nationalgeographic.com/news/2016/11/ bacteria-tiny-microscopic-shapes/

Take a closer look at some germs and other microorganisms under the microscope.

– Index –